COLOSSIANS &

PHILEMON:

DISPENSATIONALLY CONSIDERED

A GRACE EXPOSITIONAL COMMENTARY

SECOND EDITION

DR. DAVID ALAN GREENE

GraceWord Publishing, LLC
www.gracewordpublishing.com
U.S.A.

GRACEWORD PUBLISHING

Contents

To My Daughter Karla

Who Is Christ?

He is the image of the invisible God,
the firstborn of every creature:
For by Christ were all things created,
that are in heaven, and that are in earth,
visible and invisible,
whether they be thrones, or dominions,
or principalities, or powers:
all things were created by Christ,
and for Christ:
And Christ is before all things,
and by Christ all things consist.

- Apostle Paul

Acknowledgements

To my friends and family, thank you for your words of encouragement. There are too many to list by name, but you know who you are. There is one individual who worked with me during the editing process. I owe a special thanks to Winnie Stearns and Frances Greene.

Introduction

It is my custom to present readers with a summary of dispensational right division. It is the way to understand the Word of God as Paul instructed Timothy. (*cf.* 2 Tim. 2:15.) It would be a disadvantage for some readers to jump into studying the book of Colossians without this explanation. Therefore, we will cover some preliminary ground.

The letter to the Colossians is one of thirteen epistles written by the Apostle Paul. Each letter was written to a group of believers or individuals such as Philemon, Titus, and Timothy. All of them, except for the letter to the Romans, were written to people Paul knew personally. He had lived with some of them and taught them face to face. Therefore, most recipients of these letters had a general understanding of Paul's doctrines before receiving his letter.

His letter to those in Rome was different. Some of them who had heard Paul teach personally had relocated to the capitol city of Rome. However, many there had not personally met or heard Paul teach. They had become believers through the testimony of others. Written to provide a comprehensive foundation of doctrine upon which all his other letters are written, it is a summary of Pauline doctrine. Since his epistle to Romans is the definitive book, it is placed first in the series of his epistles.

I like to use a multi-part series of an epic story as an example. Think how difficult it would be to understand the full extent of a story by starting in season three. For this reason, I would like to provide you with the basis of the unique gospel message preached by Paul. It is important not to confuse or combined his distinct message of the Gospel of Grace with that of the other twelve apostles' Gospel of the Kingdom. He made three missionary trips to proclaim this gospel. His final trip was to Rome where he would be executed. Colossians is a letter believed to have been written while he was a prisoner in Rome awaiting his trial. It would have been written towards the end of his ministry. Although the church may have been planted by Epaphras, Paul was familiar with many of them.

The Apostle Paul preached a unique gospel message which he personally received from the Risen Savior. It was a mystery and had never been disclosed to anyone until it was disclosed to him. This gospel message was to be specifically directed to the Gentiles. In fact, Scripture states this clearly. God directed Ananias to heal Paul's blindness resulting from his confrontation with the Risen Savior on the Road to Damascus. Acts 9:3-9:

> 3 And as he journeyed, he came near Damascus: and suddenly there shined round about him a light from heaven:
> 4 And he fell to the earth, and heard a voice saying unto him, Saul, Saul, why persecutest thou me? 5 And he said, Who art thou, Lord? And the Lord said, I am Jesus whom thou persecutest: it is hard for thee to kick against the pricks.

> 6 And he trembling and astonished said, Lord, what wilt thou have me to do? And the Lord said unto him, Arise, and go into the city, and it shall be told thee what thou must do. 7 And the men which journeyed with him stood speechless, hearing a voice, but seeing no man. 8 And Saul arose from the earth; and when his eyes were opened, he saw no man: but they led him by the hand, and brought him into Damascus. 9 And he was three days without sight, and

neither did eat nor drink.

It is important for you to know that the Apostle Paul had never met Jesus during His earthly ministry. Therefore, he was not able to fulfill the requirements for the replacement of Judas as the twelfth apostle. (*cf.* Acts 1:21-26.)

We need to pay close attention to this dialogue between God and Ananias. Acts 9:10-16

> 10 **And there was a certain disciple at Damascus, named Ananias; and to him said the Lord in a vision, Ananias. And he said, Behold, I am here, Lord.** 11 **And the Lord said unto him, Arise, and go into the street which is called Straight, and enquire in the house of Judas for one called Saul, of Tarsus: for, behold, he prayeth,** 12 **And hath seen in a vision a man named Ananias coming in, and putting his hand on him, that he might receive his sight.**
>
> 13 **Then Ananias answered, Lord, I have heard by many of this man, how much evil he hath done to thy saints at Jerusalem:** 14 **And here he hath authority from the chief priests to bind all that call on**

thy name. 15 But the Lord said unto him, Go thy way: for he is a chosen vessel unto me, to bear my name before the Gentiles, and kings, and the children of Israel: 16 For I will shew him how great things he must suffer for my name's sake.

In his letter to the Galatians, another of Paul's epistles, he explains to them something he most likely shared with other believers in person. The verses below recall his second meeting with the other apostles in Jerusalem. Paul had only met Peter and James once before on his previous trip. Galatians 2:1-9:

1 Then fourteen years after I went up again to Jerusalem with Barnabas, and took Titus with me also. 2 And I went up by revelation, and communicated unto them that gospel which I preach among the Gentiles, but privately to them which were of reputation, lest [for fear that] by any means I should run, or had run, in vain. 3 But neither Titus, who was with me, being a Greek, was compelled to be circumcised: 4 And that because of false brethren unawares brought in, who came in privily to spy

out our liberty which we have in Christ Jesus, that they might bring us into bondage: 5 To whom we gave place by subjection, no, not for an hour; that the truth of the gospel might continue with you.

6 But of these who seemed to be somewhat [of importance], (whatsoever they were, it maketh no matter to me: God accepteth no man's person:) for they who seemed to be somewhat in conference added nothing to me:

7 But contrariwise, when they saw that the gospel of the uncircumcision was committed unto me, as the gospel of the circumcision was unto Peter; 8 (For he that wrought effectually in Peter to the apostleship of the circumcision, the same was mighty in me toward the Gentiles:) 9 And when James, Cephas, and John, who seemed to be pillars, perceived the grace that was given unto me, they gave to me and Barnabas the right hands of fellowship; that we should go unto the heathen, and they unto the circumcision.

This meeting took place prior to his writing to the Colossians.

Paul provides us with a concise statement of this gospel. Notice the use of the definite article "the" when he refers to the gospel *wherein ye stand* as the basis of their salvation. 1 Corinthians 15:1-4:

> 1 **Moreover, brethren, I declare unto you <u>the</u> gospel which I preached unto you, which also ye have received, and wherein ye stand; 2 By which also ye are saved, if ye keep in memory what I preached unto you, unless ye have believed in vain.**

> 3 <u>**For I delivered unto you first of all that which I also received,**</u> **[1] how that Christ died for our sins according to the scriptures; 4 [2] And that he was buried, and [3] that he rose again the third day according to the scriptures:**

See the simplicity of the Gospel of Grace. The gospel consisted of Christ's death on the Cross, His burial, and His resurrection. Believing in this is the basis for our salvation. Jesus Christ accomplished it all for us. This leaves *us* with nothing *to do*.

Paul makes clear the sufficiency of Christ's completed work on the Cross. He does this by making clear that nothing else can be added. This is perhaps one of the most quoted of Paul's verses. Ephesians 2:8-9:

> 8 **For by grace are ye saved through faith; and that not of yourselves: it is the gift of God: 9 Not of works, lest [for fear that] any man should boast.**

In his letter to the Galatians, he chastised some for adding works as a requirement for salvation in addition to what the Savior had already done. Many are still doing this today! To the Colossians, he wrote about their adding philosophies of men to the gospel by which they were saved.

Paul's gospel message is different from that of the Twelve. In Galatians 1, he affirms that he did not receive it from the other apostles or from any other man. He received it directly from the Risen Savior. Galatians 1:11-12:

> 11 **But I certify you, brethren, that the gospel which was preached of [from] me is not after [from] man. 12 For I neither received it of man, neither was I**

taught it, but by the revelation of Jesus Christ.

Why Paul? I asked my Methodist pastor, when I was growing up, why he did not preach from Paul's letters. He told me that it was because Paul had persecuted the Church and, therefore, he shunned him. Here is Paul's view on this. Verses 13-17:

> 13 For ye have heard of my conversation [manner of living] in time past in the Jews' religion, how that beyond measure I persecuted the church of God, and wasted it: 14 And profited in the Jews' religion above many my equals in mine own nation, being more exceedingly zealous of the traditions of my fathers.

> 15 But when it pleased God, who separated me from my mother's womb, and called me by his grace, 16 To reveal his Son in [to] me, that I might preach him among the heathen[Gentiles]; immediately I conferred not with flesh and blood [any man]: 17 Neither went I up to Jerusalem to them which were apostles before me; but [instead] I went into Arabia, and [later] returned again unto Damascus.

God set Paul a part for a special ministry to the Gentiles. That did not mean that the offer of the Gospel of Grace was not also open to the Jews. It is available to everyone but effective for only those who believe. Paul refers to faith or the act of believing throughout his epistles. Here is one last point I would like to make. This will help those new to this concept that Paul is different from the other twelve apostles. Find a large jumbo paper clip. Beginning with the last page of Acts and ending with the first page of Hebrews place the paper clip over the pages in between. The books contained within the paper clip should start with Romans and end with Philemon. These are the thirteen epistles written by Paul.

In the last chapter of Acts, immediately before Paul's first book, there is a meeting recorded. It happened while Paul was incarcerated in Rome. He called the local Jewish leaders to meet with him. (*cf.* Acts 28:16-30.) After reasoning with them at great length, they left debating amongst themselves. At that point, Paul makes a declaration. It is recorded in Acts 28:28:

28 **Be it known therefore unto you, that the salvation of God is sent unto the Gentiles, and that they will hear it.**

This ends the portion of Scripture which precedes Paul's epistles. Now, let's look at the other side.

If you turn to the portion of Scripture which follows Paul's epistles, the first book you come to is Hebrews. Are you starting to see a pattern here? The message Paul brings is directed to the Gentiles and called the Gospel of Grace. *Grace* means *gift*. Having *faith* means *believing what God said*. So, salvation from this message means believing that God is graciously offering salvation as a gift to anyone who will believe. And, Christ paid the price in full!

I would like you to see something else before we move on. There is another book that is not one of Paul's letters. It follows after the book of Hebrews. I was teaching a Bible study and explaining salvation by grace through faith when someone interrupted me. "Hey, what about 'faith without works is dead?!'" He was speaking about the verses in James. So, we all turned and read the verses in James 2:18-20:

> 18 **Yea, a man may say, Thou hast faith, and I have works: shew me thy faith without thy works, and I will shew thee my faith by my works. 19 Thou believest that there is one God; thou doest well: the devils also believe, and tremble. 20 But wilt thou know, O vain man, that**

faith without works is dead?

He confirmed these were the verses of which he was speaking. Then, I directed the group to turn to the beginning of the book of James. I read aloud the salutation from verse 1:

> 1 **James, a servant of God and of the Lord Jesus Christ, <u>to the twelve tribes which are scattered abroad</u>, greeting.**

James is writing to the twelve tribes of Israel scattered throughout the nations. Being a bit cheeky, I asked him from which tribe he came. In other words, James is writing to the children of Israel — *the twelve tribes which are scattered abroad.* All the books which follow Paul's epistles, from Hebrews to Revelation, are written to Israel; not the Gentiles.

GraceWord Publishing has excellent books which explain this division in greater detail. The book entitled Letters to Theophilus is a summary of the entire Bible from Genesis to Revelation. It provides an understanding of the Bible's framework. There are also other online resources. I was first introduced to rightly dividing by watching online YouTube videos and pre-recorded television shows by Les Feldick, a Midwest rancher who taught many how to understand and enjoy their Bibles. Les is with the Lord now, but his video classes are only 30 minutes long and worth the time.

Now, with this brief introduction to Paul and his unique gospel message, we are ready to begin our study of the books of Colossians and Philemon.

1

Controversy At Colossae

The ancient city of Colossae was located in present-day Turkey. The distance between Colossae and Ephesus is approximately 120 miles, an easy two-day journey for Paul. Laodicea, another city, was less than ten miles away. In fact, all of the seven churches listed in Revelation are in this same region. The website www.jesuswalk.com has an excellent map showing these locations. It can be seen at:

https://www.jesuswalk.com/colossians/images/sw-turkey-map-outline-468x387.gif

Colossae grew into an important city from its beginning in the 5th century BC. Later, due to the relocation of a major commerce route, its importance had begun to diminish by the time of Paul. As an established Roman city, it was filled with pagan religions, Jewish believers, and philosophies of men. This city was destroyed by an earthquake approximately 1100 AD and the citizens were forced to move to nearby cities. This is the historical context of the group of grace believers at Colossae. It was these effects of the prevalence of pagan religions and philosophies that made it necessary for Paul to write the Colossians a letter of instruction.

This information is important as it helps us understand the background of these believers. As with all believers, their problems resulted from their circumstances. This will not be a study on false teachings, other than to point out that anything contrary to the Bible is wrong. In a letter to Timothy, Paul writes in 1 Timothy 4:1-2:

> 1 **Now the Spirit speaketh expressly, that in the latter times some shall depart from the faith, <u>giving heed to seducing spirits, and doctrines of devils</u>; 2 <u>Speaking lies in hypocrisy</u>; having their conscience seared with a hot iron;**

Similarly, here is another verse from Colossians 2:8:

8 Beware lest [for fear that] any man spoil you through philosophy and vain deceit, after the tradition of men, after the rudiments of the world, and not after Christ.

As the Apostle to the Gentiles, his duty and charge is to care for those saved by grace. It was his instruction which led them to believe and accept God's gift of salvation. He continues to pray for and watch over them like a father in their faith. When he sees the train is going off the tracks of sound biblical teaching, he admonishes them in a letter. Some letters include chastisement, but are always written with love for the believers.

The greatest threat to these believers is from the inclusion of false doctrines. Satan is the father of lies. He took the truth which God gave to Adam in the garden and altered it. Remember this: truth altered is no longer truth. This has been the case since the first lie was recorded in Genesis 3:4-5:

4 And the serpent said unto the woman, Ye shall not surely die: 5 For God doth know that in the day ye eat thereof, then your eyes shall be opened, and ye shall

be as gods, knowing good and evil.

We are told that Satan as "the serpent was more subtle than any beast of the field" (Gen. 3:1). Adam and Eve, the progenitors of all mankind, listened to his lie. The results were both catastrophic and far-reaching.

Gnosticism was a cultish obsession with many devotees and began before the birth of Christ. The word *gnosis* comes from the Greek word for *knowledge*. Its origin was the philosophies of men and the religion of false gods. It centered around the concept of special spiritual knowledge which was given to those who participated in cults. These cults were dedicated to achieving higher spiritual awareness. The use of the words "divine human spark" was used then as it is now and implies an inner god in mankind. The lie of the serpent was, ". . . your eyes shall be opened, and ye shall be as gods . . ." (Gen. 3:5). Gnosticism promises its adherents will receive a return to their divine nature which exists as a "spark" within mankind. It also teaches that the physical flesh is evil while the spiritual is the divine. Think about this for a moment. Today, many churches preach *the knowledge of man* which is contrary to *the wisdom of God*.

4

What impact did this gnostic philosophy have upon the believers in Colossae? It attacked the deity of Christ. Gnosticism taught that the body or flesh was evil. This created a problem. If the flesh is evil and Jesus came in the flesh, then He is either not God or He really was not in the flesh. Their teaching was that He only *appeared* to be in the flesh. This alters the truth. Here is just one example that this is contrary to Scripture. Romans 1:3-4:

> 3 **Concerning his Son Jesus Christ our Lord, <u>which was made of the seed of David according to the flesh;</u> 4 And declared to be the Son of God with power, according to the spirit of holiness, <u>by the resurrection from the dead</u>:**

This teaching is also contrary to the Gospel of the Kingdom taught by the twelve. 1 John 4:3:

> 3 **And every spirit that confesseth not that <u>Jesus Christ is come in the flesh</u> is not of God: and <u>this is that spirit of antichrist</u>, whereof ye have heard that it should come; and even now already is it in the world.**

Christ is a man, a descendent of King David. He is a real Person who suffered like others even to death on the Cross. As the result of this death, God raised Him from the dead because of His righteousness.

Theologians struggled to define God which is describing the most complex and infinite. They resolved to leave it as a matter of faith with the following truths. Their explanation is called the *hypostatic union:* the connection between the divine nature of the Lord Jesus Christ and the human nature of Jesus of Nazareth. Jesus Christ is both fully-God and fully-Man. He is a true person physically, mentally, and emotionally. He is also fully divine. These two natures co-exist in one Person. In his letter to the Philippians, Paul writes in verses 2:6-8:

> **6 Who, being in the form of God, thought it not robbery to be equal with God: 7 But made himself of no reputation, and took upon him the form of a servant, and was made in the likeness of men: 8 And being found in fashion as a man, he humbled himself, and became obedient unto death, even the death of the cross.**

In his letter to the Colossians, Paul refutes the philosophical claims by presenting the unadulterated truth–the Word of God. Sometimes viewed as a basic truth according to biblical doctrine, it is often misconstrued. Anyone who argues for the superiority of God the Father and the inferiority of His Son, is teaching the false doctrines of men. With this general introduction, we are ready to move on and, through his letter, let Paul speak for himself.

2

Colossians 1

As with all of his letters, Paul begins with his salutation identifying himself and Timothy as the senders. Acknowledging his apostleship of the Gospel of Grace, he reminds them of the grace given to them and the peace from God and His Son. Colossians 1:1-2:

> 1 **Paul, an apostle of Jesus Christ by the will of God, and Timotheus our brother,** 2 **To the saints and faithful brethren in Christ which are at Colosse: Grace be unto you, and peace, from God our Father and the Lord Jesus Christ.**

It was his custom to maintain communication with the groups of grace believers. He is thankful for their faith and the way they show love for their fellow believers. Paul include the Colossians in his prayers. Verses 3-4:

> 3 **We give thanks to God and the Father of our Lord Jesus Christ, praying always for you, 4 Since we heard of your faith in Christ Jesus, and of the love which ye have to all the saints,**

He gets right into the point of his letter by reminding them of the hope they have when they believed the Gospel of Grace. Verse 5:

> 5 **For the hope which is laid up for you in heaven, whereof ye heard before in the word of the truth of the gospel;**

This gospel was new and different from anything people had heard. It was spreading by word of mouth throughout the known world. Verse 6:

> 6 **Which is come unto you, as it is in all the world; and bringeth forth fruit, as it doth also in you, since the day ye heard of it, and knew the grace of God in truth:**

There were individuals who carried messages

between the churches and Paul. Many of them were well known by the churches and he frequently mentions these individual in his letters by name. It is believed that Epaphras was the missionary who first brought the gospel message to Colossae. Verses 7-8:

> 7 **As ye also learned of Epaphras our dear fellowservant, who is for you a faithful minister of Christ; 8 Who also declared unto us your love in the Spirit.**

Concerning their expression of love in the Spirit, Paul writes in his letter that he is praying for them also. He constantly encourages believers to *be filled with the knowledge of his will in all wisdom and spiritual understanding*. Verse 9:

> 9 **For this cause we also, since the day we heard it, do not cease to pray for you, and to desire that ye might be filled with the knowledge of his will in all wisdom and spiritual understanding;**

This knowledge and understanding is only possible by studying the Word of Truth rightly divided (2 Tim. 2:15).

Paul is an apostle appointed by the Lord Jesus Christ and God to proclaim the Gospel of Grace.

(See Gal 1:1.) He was charged with the teaching and care of those believers saved by grace and who must walk worthy of *His Calling.* Believers are to bring forth fruit in the same way a healthy fruit tree produces fruit. However, in their case, this fruit is actually the yield of Christ Who resides in them. This is not works in order to achieve or maintain their salvation. Paul makes this clear in Romans 11:6:

> 6 **And <u>if by grace, then is it no more of works:</u> otherwise grace is no more grace. But <u>if it be of works, then is it no more grace</u>: otherwise work is no more work.**

He desires that they ". . . might be filled with the knowledge of His will in all wisdom and spiritual understanding" (v. 9). Again, this source of knowledge and wisdom can only be the Word of God.

He repeats his desire that they act according to their position *in Christ.* Fruit is produced because of their healthy relationship with Jesus Christ, their Savior. Verse 10:

> 10 **That ye might walk worthy of the Lord unto all pleasing, being fruitful in every good work, and increasing in the knowledge of God;**

We must be confident in the Word of God, planting both feet solidly upon that foundation. Our faith, being strong, will not waiver regardless of circumstance. We can patiently endure any hardships or challenges that befall us, and do so joyfully. Verses 11-12:

> **11 Strengthened with all might, according to his glorious power, unto all patience and longsuffering with joyfulness; 12 Giving thanks unto the Father, which hath made us meet to be partakers of the inheritance of the saints in light:**

Let us stop for a moment and consider what he refers to as *the inheritance of the saints*. This is important as he also mentions it in Ephesians 1:17-19:

> **17 That the God of our Lord Jesus Christ, the Father of glory, may give unto you the spirit of wisdom and revelation in the knowledge of him:**

> **18 <u>The eyes of your understanding being enlightened; that ye may know what is the hope of his calling, and what the riches of the glory of his inheritance in the saints,</u>**

19 And what is the exceeding greatness of his power to us-ward who believe, according to the working of his mighty power,

The Spirit inspired the writers of the Bible. The word *inspired* means *God-breathed*. In like manner, those who wish to understand God's Word must also involve the Holy Spirit. This Spirit is resident in all believers and it is He Who will *illuminate* the Word of God for us. Look at the reference above in verse 18. He uses the word *enlightened*. In other words, the meaning of God's Word is brought to light or our understanding by the Holy Spirit.

Through His Son, God has taken us from darkness, not knowing Him at all, to being saved and placed *in Christ*. Following His resurrection, our Risen Lord is now seated beside God in heaven. We must always remember what He has done for us and give thanks to God the Father. Paul puts this to words in Colossians 1:13-14:

13 Who hath delivered us from the power of darkness, and hath translated us into the kingdom of his dear Son: 14 In whom we have redemption through his blood, even the forgiveness of sins:

He uses this as an introduction to clarify the deity of Jesus Christ. He wants them to know the extent of the deity of Christ. Christ is fully God! Verses 15-16:

> 15 **Who is the image of the invisible God, the firstborn of every creature:** 16 **For by him were all things created, that are in heaven, and that are in earth, visible and invisible, whether they be thrones, or dominions, or principalities, or powers: all things were created by him, and for him:**

Christ is the visible image of the invisible God. At the very beginning of the Bible, we are given a fact. Genesis 1:1:

> 1 **In the beginning <u>God created the heaven and the earth.</u>**

From this, we can clearly see that God created the heaven and the earth. Now, Paul tells us in the above verses it was Christ Who created the heaven and the earth. He created all things *that are in heaven, and that are in earth.* Considering that the Bible is our only source of truth, this must bring us to a logical conclusion. If God is the Creator, and Christ is the creator, then God and Christ are One in the same. Charles Wesley must have considered this truth when he penned the lyrics to "And Can It Be." He wrote the words, *Amazing love! How can it be that Thou, my God, shouldst die for me!*

Did you notice that in the above verses Christ is referred to as *the firstborn of every creature?* Some people use this verse to deduce that Christ did not always exist. This would be a false interpretation because Christ as God has always existed. Here is the explanation: Christ is the *firstborn* from the dead. He was the first to be resurrected by God. If Christ is the visible image of God, then it must have been Christ Who showed Himself when Moses requested the God reveal Himself to him. Exodus 33:18-23:

> 18 **And he[Moses] said, I beseech thee, shew me thy glory. 19 And he said, I will make all my goodness pass before thee, and I will proclaim the name of the LORD before thee; and <u>[I] will be gracious to whom I will be gracious, and will shew mercy on whom I will shew mercy.</u>**
>
> 20 **And he said, Thou canst not see my face: for there shall no man see me, and live. 21 And the LORD said, Behold, there is a place by me, and thou shalt stand upon a rock:**

22 And it shall come to pass, while my glory passeth by, that I will put thee in a cleft of the rock, and will cover thee with my hand while I pass by: 23 And I will take away mine hand, and thou shalt see my back parts: but my face shall not be seen.

Moses saw only in part what we shall someday see face to face. 1 Corinthians 13:12:

12 For now we see through a glass, darkly; but then face to face: now I know in part; but then shall I know even as also I am known.

Paul continues his description of the Risen Savior. Here he states the fact about Christ being the *firstborn from the dead.* Colossians 1:17-18:

17 And <u>he is before all things,</u> and <u>by him all things consist.</u> 18 And he is <u>the head of the body,</u> the church: who is the beginning, <u>the firstborn from the dead;</u> that in all things he might have the preeminence.

There is a great plan and purpose in effect. God has a plan to completely restore fallen Creation. God will achieve that plan through Christ so that *in all things He might have the preeminence!*

Keep this thought in mind as Paul continues with verses 19-20:

> 19 **For it pleased the Father that in him [Christ] should all fulness dwell;**
>
> 20 **And, having made peace through the blood of his cross, by him [Christ] to reconcile all things unto himself [God]; by him [Christ], I say, whether they be things in earth, or things in heaven.**

Paul will again confirm this in verses 2:10-11:

> 10 **That at the name of Jesus every knee should bow, of things in heaven, and things in earth, and things under the earth;**
>
> 11 **And that every tongue should confess that Jesus Christ is Lord, to the glory of God the Father.**

Those saved by grace through faith are only one of the many facets which will comprise this restoration of Creation. All this is to the glory to God!

Paul now writes about the grace believers. He again compares their current state with that of their past. Notice the change in position. Verses 1:21-22:

> **21 And you, that were sometime [ago] alienated and enemies in your mind by wicked works, yet now hath he reconciled 22 In the body of his flesh through death, to present you holy and unblameable and unreproveable in his sight:**

It is through Paul's personal sacrifice that we have been reconciled to God. This was only possible through the finished work of Jesus Christ–through His death, burial, and resurrection!

Like us today, the Colossians found themselves in difficult situations. Paul encourages all believers to continue in their faith and not be moved from the promise of salvation. Verse 23:

> **23 If ye continue in the faith grounded and settled, and [then] be not moved away from the hope of the gospel, which ye have heard, and which was preached to every creature which is under heaven; whereof I Paul am made a minister;**

Therefore, once we believe the gospel of our salvation, we must not be removed from it. We must hold onto this hope. This same gospel which they believed was being preached throughout the then-known world. This message is not only being heard from Paul, the Apostle of the Gospel of Grace, but also from those who have heard it and are now sharing it with others.

Paul suffered greatly to advance and defend his message of grace. He remained a faithful servant of the Lord Jesus Christ throughout his life. He counts his sufferings and afflictions worthy for grace believers who are the church–the Body of Christ. Verse 24:

> 24 **Who now rejoice in my sufferings for you, and fill up that which is behind of the afflictions of Christ in my flesh for his body's sake, which is the church:**

God temporarily suspended the Dispensation of Law for an unspecified period of time. The present dispensation is called the Dispensation of Grace. The Jews had rejected their Messiah. Stephen made an impassioned speech before the rulers of Israel. He was charged with being a blasphemer and immediately brought outside to be stoned. Their rejection precipitated his temporary suspension. At his stoning, we were introduced to a Pharisee named Saul.

Saul persecuted the new believers of the Kingdom Gospel until his conversion on the Road to Damascus. For three years following that divine confrontation, Paul received instruction from the Risen Lord and was given a message to be delivered to the Gentiles. This parenthetical interruption of the Dispensation of Law begins with Paul's conversion. He was the first to be saved by grace and made a pattern for others to follow. (*cf.* 1 Tim. 1:16.) The Age of Grace will end at the Rapture with the removal of all grace believers. Following that historic moment, the remaining seven years of the Dispensation of Law will resume. With this information the following verse will make sense. Remember, the grace believers in Colossae are predominantly Gentiles. Verse 25:

25 **Whereof I am made a minister, according to the dispensation of God which is given to me for you [Gentiles], to fulfil the word of God;**

Paul's gospel of good news for the Gentiles is unique from all the other apostles. What the Risen Lord revealed to him was never before mentioned of in Scripture. Not only was it hidden from men, but it was also hidden from the angelic host, the powers and principalities that govern this fallen world. The revelation of this *mystery* which was hidden in God was directed to the Gentiles and would complete the restoration of God's Creation. God's original plan and purpose for Israel remains unchanged. Verses 26-27:

> 26 Even the <u>mystery which hath been hid from ages and from generations</u>, but now is made manifest [known] to his saints: 27 To whom <u>God would make known what is the riches of the glory of this mystery among the Gentiles</u>; which is Christ in you, the hope of glory:

Note that *the hope of glory* to which Paul is referring is the culmination of the Dispensation of Grace. It is the Rapture or *His Calling* of those who chose to accept and believe his gracious offer of salvation.

It is this glorious *Gospel of the Grace of God* which Paul received that is now preached through others who have themselves been saved. This Gospel of Grace is directed to the Gentiles in the same manner as the promises of the Gospel of the Kingdom are directed to the children of Israel (*cf.* Romans 15:8.) But now, this message of salvation by grace through faith to the Gentiles is also available to any Jew who chooses to believe. In this present age, everyone can be saved by grace through faith. Verses 28-29:

28 [Christ] Whom we preach, warning every man, and teaching every man in all wisdom; [so] that we may present every man perfect in Christ Jesus:

29 Whereunto I also labour, striving according to his working, which worketh in me mightily.

Christ works through those who belong to Him. Paul constantly worked to advance the message of the Gospel of the Grace of God to everyone who would listen.

3

Colossians 2

Paul was a missionary preacher. He traveled through the Roman Empire preaching the Gospel of Grace. Sometimes he would stay long enough to be confident of their doctrinal foundation and establish teachers. After he left, he would communicate with them through letters or messengers. Like a parent who agonizes over a child now on his own, Paul continues to worry about those who accepted the gospel message. Colossians 2:1:

> 1 **For I would that ye knew what great conflict I have for you, and for them at Laodicea, and for as many as have not seen my face in the flesh;**

This message is often referred to, by Paul, as *my gospel*. It is also referred to as *the mystery of God* until it was revealed to him by the Lord Jesus Christ. Romans 16:25:

> 25 Now to him that is of power to stablish you according to <u>my gospel</u>, and the preaching of Jesus Christ, <u>according to the revelation of the mystery, which was kept secret since the world began</u>,

Paul will often write to grace believers about the unity in the Spirit. Think of a small group of people who hold to this totally unique Gospel of Grace. Its teachings contradict everything the rest of the world believes. Their only true means of support are those who also hold to the same gospel. Together they are clinging to Christ like a life raft in a sea of worldly wickedness. No one other than those saved by the same gospel would understand, encourage, or support them. Verses 2-3:

> 2 That <u>their hearts might be comforted, being knit together in love</u>, and unto all riches of the full assurance of understanding, to the acknowledgement of the mystery of God, and of the Father, and of Christ; 3 In whom are hid all the treasures of wisdom and knowledge.

Their mission is to fully understand the riches of

Christ and make Christ known to others.

The enemy uses those who are of the world to entice these believers away from Paul's teachings. He warns them of this especially while he is not with them in person to protect them. Verses 4-5:

> 4 **And this I say, lest [for fear that] any man should beguile you with enticing words. 5 For though I be absent in the flesh, yet am I with you in the spirit, joying and beholding your order, and the stedfastness of your faith in Christ.**

He encourages them to remain steadfast or unshakeable in their faith in Christ. Not only should they remain devoted, but they should also act worthy of *His Calling*. Verse 6:

> 6 **As ye have therefore received Christ Jesus the Lord, so walk ye in him: 7 Rooted and built up in him, and stablished in the faith, as ye have been taught, abounding therein with thanksgiving.**

The Bible is often referred to as *the Word of God*. The Apostle John tells us this in John 1:1:

1 In the beginning was the Word, and the Word was with God, and the Word was God.

In order for any believer to be *rooted and built up in him, and stablished in the faith,* they must immerse themselves in *the Word of God!* Christ is *the Word of God* and the *Word of God* is the Bible. This is the only means by which they can prevent being beguiled by false teachings of the world. Verse 8:

8 Beware lest [for fear that] any man spoil you through philosophy and vain deceit, after the tradition of men, after the rudiments of the world, and not after Christ.

Having mentioned Christ, Paul once again affirms His divine attributes. Verse 9:

9 For in him [Christ] dwelleth all the fulness of the Godhead bodily. 10 And <u>ye are complete in him,</u> which [Who] is the head of all principality and power:

Once someone is saved by grace through faith without works, they are sealed by the Holy Spirit. They are then immediately placed *in Christ.* Paul's letter to the Ephesians goes into this in great depth. As grace believers we have eternal security *in Christ*. The work necessary for our salvation was completed on our behalf by Christ on the Cross. Friend, we were redeemed or bought back by His precious blood. Being bought by His blood they now belong to Him and *are complete in Him*.

Paul makes a reference to a procedure which was a physical mark on all Hebrew males when they are eight days old. It is the sign of the Abrahamic Covenant and it is a distinction made in the flesh as a remembrance of that covenant. Grace believers are not compelled to do this because they are not under the Law. However, Paul makes a comparison in verse 11:

> 11 **In whom [Christ] also ye are circumcised with the circumcision made without hands, in putting off the body of the sins of the flesh by the circumcision of Christ:**

Circumcision is the cutting away of flesh and we, who are still in our mortal bodies, must put off our flesh. Think of those words for a moment as we consider that, when we were saved, we were spiritually placed *in Christ*. Yet, our physical bodies or flesh remained here on earth until the appropriate time.

Our redemption is in two parts. First, we are saved spiritually and placed *in Christ*. We remain in our physical bodies, or flesh, until the redemption of our bodies. You may have noticed the words *His Calling*. This refers to the calling of *His Body unto Himself* which is the Rapture. Again, our spiritual body is *in Christ* which is in the heavenlies. This is the fulfillment of our redemption which is guaranteed. Paul explains this in Ephesians 1:13-14:

> 13 **In whom ye also trusted, after that ye heard the word of truth, the gospel of your salvation: in whom also after that ye believed, ye were [immediately] sealed with that holy Spirit of promise,**
>
> 14 **Which is the earnest of our inheritance until the redemption of the purchased possession, unto the praise of his glory.**

The word *earnest* is a legal term still used in real estate transactions. It is the deposit which guarantees the completion of the transaction. The purchase agreement was sealed and there was an earnest deposit given which guarantees the fulfillment of the promise–the Holy Spirit?

The most concise statement of what comprises the Gospel of Grace is found in 1 Corinthians 15:1-4:

> 1 **Moreover, brethren, I declare unto you <u>the gospel</u> which I preached unto you, which also ye have received, and wherein ye stand; 2 By which also ye are saved, if ye keep in memory what I preached unto you, unless ye have believed in vain.**

> 3 **For I delivered unto you first of all that which I also received, how that [1] Christ died for our sins according to the scriptures; 4 And that [2] he was buried, and that [3] he rose again the third day according to the scriptures:**

This is the very essence of the Gospel of Grace. Everything that was needed to appease the wrath of God towards mankind was completed by Christ. He did it all! Paul is adamant that nothing else can be added by mankind without making it another gospel which is not a gospel at all! (*cf.* Gal. 1:6-9.)

It is about this death, burial, and resurrection of Christ that Paul writes in Colossians 2:12-13:

12 Buried with him in baptism, wherein also ye are risen with him through the faith of the operation of God, who hath raised him from the dead.

13 And you, being dead in your sins and the uncircumcision of your flesh, hath he quickened [made alive] together with him, having forgiven you all trespasses;

The Gospel of Grace is very simple. It is its simplicity that causes the wise to say that it is *foolishness!*

Friend, this is too important to gloss over. We need to look at three places where Paul specifically writes about this *foolishness.*

1 Corinthians 1:18-25:

18 For the preaching of the cross is to them that perish foolishness; but unto us which are saved it is the power of God.

19 For it is written, I [God] will destroy the wisdom of the wise, and will bring to nothing the understanding of the prudent.

20 Where is the wise? where is the scribe? where is the disputer of this world? hath not God made foolish the wisdom of this world?

21 For after that in the wisdom of God the world by [its own] wisdom knew not God, it pleased God by the foolishness of preaching to save them that believe. 22 For the Jews require a sign, and the Greeks [Gentiles] seek after wisdom:

23 But we preach Christ crucified, unto the Jews a stumblingblock, and unto the Greeks foolishness; 24 But unto them which are called [believe], both Jews and Greeks, Christ the power of God, and the wisdom of God.

25 Because the foolishness of God is wiser than men; and the weakness of God is stronger than men.

1 Corinthians 2:14:

14 But the natural [unsaved] man receiveth not the things of the Spirit of God: for they are foolishness unto him:

neither can he know them, because they [these truths] are spiritually discerned.

1 Corinthians 3:18-20:

18 Let no man deceive himself. If any man among you seemeth to be wise in this world, <u>let him become a fool, that he may be wise.</u>

19 For <u>the wisdom of this world is fool-ishness</u> with God. For it is written, He taketh the wise in their own craftiness. 20 And again, The Lord knoweth the thoughts of the wise, that they are vain.

Let those who appear to be wise in *the wisdom of this world* become fools so that they may understand *the wisdom of God*. There are few churches today that preach *the wisdom of God*.

Paul makes something very clear. Those who are saved by God's grace are *not under the Law*. The *wisdom of this world* would have people do something so that they contribute to their salvation. This wisdom of the world cannot be applied to salvation by grace. It is either fully by works or fully by grace–the gift of God. Galatians 2:16:

16 Knowing that a man is <u>not justified</u> <u>by the works of the law, but by the faith</u> <u>of Jesus Christ</u>, even we have believed in Jesus Christ, that we might be <u>justi-</u> <u>fied by the faith [faithfulness] of Christ</u>, and <u>not by the works of the law</u>: for <u>by</u> <u>the works of the law shall no flesh be</u> <u>justified</u>.

This is the very heart of Paul's Gospel of Grace.

Now, let us continue with Colossians 2:14:

14 Blotting out the handwriting of ordinances [rules] that was against us, which was contrary to [condemned] us, and [He] took it out of the way, nailing it to his cross;

Prior to God revealing the Gospel of Grace to Paul, it had been a *mystery*. Not only was it a mystery to mankind, but it was also hidden from the heavenly host. This included those that are the opposition. So, when it was revealed to Paul, it was also made known to them. The opposition had no idea the impact of this on their plans to circumvent God. When they slew God's Son, they believed they had won. Now that the *mystery* was revealed, it showed everyone God has already won the battle.

35

The victory is only made possible by the Cross! Verse 15:

15 And having spoiled principalities and powers, he made a shew of them openly, triumphing over them in it.

Paul refers to the opposition as *principalities and powers*. God's Son having fulfilled all righteous according to the Law was declared righteous by God. Raising Him from the dead, He also raised those who, through faith, would be placed *in Him*. Paul summaries the enormity of this event. 1 Corinthians 15:55-57:

55 O death, where is thy sting? O grave, where is thy victory? 56 The sting of death is sin; and the strength of sin is the law.

57 But thanks be to God, which [Who] <u>giveth us the victory through our Lord Jesus Christ</u>.

Some things never change. As it was then, so is it today. People feel they have the right to judge others and condemn them. This applies especially to what is eaten or drunk; even judging others concerning minor holiday observances. Colossians 2:16-17:

16 Let no man therefore judge you in meat [what you eat], or in [what you] drink, or in respect [to observance] of an holyday, or of the new moon, or of the sabbath days: **17** Which are a shadow of things to come; but the body is of Christ.

Grace believers are the Body of Christ. At the beginning of this letter, Paul writes that *Christ is in us* and that is *our blessed hope* of glory and concerns the Rapture. Colossians 1:27:

27 To whom [grace believers] God would make known what is <u>the riches of the glory of this mystery</u> among the Gentiles; <u>which [Who] is Christ in you</u>, the hope of glory:

The revelation of this *mystery* caused quite a stir in the spiritual realm. Enough so that it became the focus of the opposition to prevent or pervert the Gospel of Grace. Therefore, most of Paul's letters deal with issues concerning the perversion of the simple message of salvation by grace. Verse 18:

18 Let no man beguile [deceive] you of your reward in a voluntary humility and [as well as] worshipping of angels,

intruding into those things which he [this man] hath not seen, vainly puffed up by his [own] fleshly mind,

There are many in pulpits who have assumed leadership over believers. They voluntarily exhibit humility when people are watching them, but enjoy the devotion they receive and obedience shown to them. They beguile or deceive others because they are puffed up in their fleshly or carnal minds.

In the Old Testament, the gods of the pagans were false gods. These fallen angels were those who, with Satan, rebelled against God. All of the angels who serve the one true God will vehemently reject worship from humans. This, no doubt, is due to fallen angels seeking worship of themselves. False teachers teach about worshipping angels, but will ignore Christ Who is the true Head of the church–the Body of Christ. Verse 19:

19 And not holding [acknowledging the authority of] the Head, from which all the body by joints and bands having nourishment ministered, and knit together, increaseth with the increase of God.

Christ, Who is the head of the Body of Christ, nourishes and builds this body of true believers. It is God Who causes it to both increase in knowledge as well as mature and grow in the faith.

Ordinances are the laws of men, the customs and traditions of men. Paul puts forth this question: If we are dead with Christ in this world, why are we subjected to the ordinances of men? This is not about governmental laws, but the ordinances established by anyone who is *vainly puffed up by his fleshly mind* (v. 18). Perhaps you can think of churches that had created their own rules and regulations which boggle the mind. It is to these ordinances that Paul refers in verses 20-22:

> 20 **Wherefore if ye be dead with Christ from the rudiments [principles] of the world, why [then], as though living in the world, are ye subject to ordinances,**
>
> 21 **(Touch not; taste not; handle not; 22 Which all are to perish with the using;) after the commandments and doctrines of men?**

For these rules and teachings are from men and not from God. These ordinances and their foolish application do nothing. They will perish along with those who teach them.

The following verse addresses vain philosophies of the world which are the invention of man. One such philosophy is asceticism which denies the body in order to attain a higher "spiritual" level. Verse 23:

23 **Which things have indeed a shew [show] of wisdom in will worship, and humility, and neglecting of the body; not in any honour to the satisfying of the flesh.**

Paul began with this warning: *let no man beguile you or deceive you of your reward.* As grace believers, we cannot lose our salvation as we never bought or paid for it. We belong to Christ. It is He Who purchased us with His blood. Therefore, we are eternally secure in Him! What Paul is referring to is our rewards; not our salvation. Paul writes about our reward in the next chapter where we will study this matter further.

4

Colossians 3

The following is a continuation from the previous chapter. We know that the gospel by which we are saved involves Christ's death, burial, and resurrection. (*cf.* 1 Cor. 15:1-4.) Now, let us apply this within a context. In verse 2:20, Paul writes *if ye be dead with Christ.* We know that when one is dead that He is buried. Therefore, we were also *buried with Christ* which is symbolically represented in water baptism. Colossians 3:1-3:

> 1 **If ye then be <u>risen with Christ</u>, [then] seek those things which are above, where Christ sitteth on the right hand of God.**
>
> 2 **Set your affection on things [which are] above, not on things on the earth.**

3 For ye are dead, and <u>your life is hid with Christ</u> in God.

As he continues, he makes reference to Christ's appearing which is not to be confused with His return. His appearing is at the Rapture when we shall receive our glorified bodies and be with Him forever. Verse 4:

4 When Christ, who is our life, shall appear, <u>then shall ye also appear with him in glory.</u>

The word "if" begins a conditional statement. Should the condition be met, a statement of the result follows the "then" clause. Those saved by grace through faith without works are *dead in Christ*, we are *buried in Christ*, and we are risen *in Christ*. Here, Paul tells us that we will also be *in Christ* when He appears in glory presenting us to the Father.

He is going to address our physical bodies by referring to members of the body such as our hands, arms, and feet. While we remain on earth, awaiting *His Calling*, we are to mortify or treat as dead the needs of our flesh. We are not to gratify our bodies with earthly pleasures. Verses 5-7:

5 Mortify therefore your members which are upon the earth; fornication, uncleanness, inordinate affection, evil concupiscence, and covetousness, which is idolatry:

6 For which things' sake the wrath of God cometh on the children of disobedience: **7** In the which [in these things] ye also walked some time [ago], when ye lived in them [these pleasures].

Each of these earthly pleasure are sought after by the desires of the flesh. We once lived in them, but now are contrary to a manner of living worthy of *His Calling*. These are part of the world to which we are now *dead in Christ*. Verses 8-9:

8 But now ye also put off all these; anger, wrath, malice, blasphemy, filthy communication out of your mouth. **9** Lie not one to another, seeing that ye have put off the old man with his deeds;

We are to put off the old man, our flesh which is now *dead in Christ*. Now, we are to live in a manner worthy of *His Calling*. We are a new creation in the image of God. He mentions this in the first chapter. It is Christ "Who is the image of the invisible God, the firstborn of every creature" (Col. 1:15). Christ is the firstborn from the dead – the first to be resurrected from the dead. We will be like Him. Verses 10-11:

> 10 **And have put on the new man, which is renewed in knowledge after the image of him that created him: 11 Where there is neither Greek nor Jew, circumcision nor uncircumcision, Barbarian, Scythian, bond nor free: but Christ is all, and in all.**

Paul writes about a *renewal* in knowledge. He defines this in Romans 12:2:

> 2 **And be not conformed to this world: but <u>be ye transformed by the renewing of your mind</u>, that ye may prove [test] what is that good, and acceptable, and perfect, will of God.**

This *renewal* is accomplished by *the renewing of your mind*–the immersion in the Word of God. The Bible is the *only* source of knowledge of God.

Knowledge can only be gained by studying the Word of God. As grace believers, God has determined in advance that we should be made into the image of His Son. How can we put this into practice? It helps when we study His Word to understand God's ultimate purpose. Romans 8:28-30:

> **28 And we know that all things work together for good to them that love God, to them who are the called according to his purpose. 29 For whom he did foreknow, <u>he also did predestinate to be conformed to the image of his Son</u>, that he might be the firstborn among many brethren.**
>
> **30 Moreover whom he did predestinate, them he also called: and whom he called, them he also justified: and whom he justified, them <u>he also glorified</u>.**

The above verse is often used to support the belief that God determined in advance those who would be saved and those who would not. This is not the case! It is important that we stop for a moment to clarify this.

Some theologians talk about God looking down *the hallway of time*. They hold that, in His sovereignty, God predestined those who would receive salvation and those who would not. However, I am going to go in another direction. I am looking up. Picture a brand-new skyscraper with two hundred and two floors. In the lobby, there is a bank of fifty elevators. There are four groups of twelve, each serving only a grouping of fifty floors each. In order words, if I wanted to go to the 45th floor, I would go to the group that services the first fifty floors. There are two remaining elevators. These two elevators are express elevators that only go to the restaurant on the top two floors. Let us assume the facts.

Continuing with this example, we could say that the architect or creator of the building *predetermined in advance* his purpose for these last two elevators. It was part of his original design even before the building came to exist. Therefore, anyone who gets on these two elevators will arrive at the architect's predetermined destination – the top two floors. However, this architect did not predetermine *who* would enter these elevators. Anyone is free to enter them by their own free will. As *the creator* of the building, he did not *predetermine* who would enter them. However, for those who do choose to enter them, their destination (the top two floors) was predetermined. Likewise, those who choose, by their own free will, to accept the Gospel of Grace, their destination has also been predetermined. Long ago, God *predetermined* that they will be *conformed to the image of his Son!*

Grace believers are blessed far beyond the gift of their salvation they received upon believing. In view of our future destiny, Paul wants us to act accordingly. In other words, in a manner worthy of *His Calling.* Verses 12-15:

> 12 **Put on therefore, as the elect of God, holy and beloved, bowels of [in thy inner most parts] mercies, kindness, humbleness of mind, meekness, longsuffering;**
>
> 13 **Forbearing one another, and forgiving one another, if any man have a quarrel against any: even as Christ forgave you, so also do ye.** 14 **And above all these things put on charity, which is the bond of perfectness.** 15 **And let the peace of God rule in your hearts, to the which also ye are called in one body; and be ye thankful.**

Let us stop for a moment and consider the word *elect* used above. This word has a specific meaning. It means *chosen.* For example, the president elect is the president chosen by votes. Abraham was chosen by God and, therefore, he is God's elect. This also applies to Israel who, as children of Abraham, are God's *chosen* people. You may ask, "How does this apply to grace believers saved by the Gospel of Grace?"

The Lord Jesus Christ is God's *Elect* and the Seed of Abraham. We were chosen *in Him* before the foundation of the world. The moment we believed and were saved by grace through faith, we were placed *in Christ.* Like those who, of their own free will entered the express elevator to the top floor, they were the ones whom God predetermined would arrive at the top floor. He planned all this in advance. He predetermined the destination of those who are in the elevator. Therefore, being *in Christ,* Paul refers to grace believers as *the elect of God.*

Throughout his letters, Paul continually encourages the believers to get into God's Word. Remember, the Word of God is Christ. The depth of our relationship with our Savior can be measured by our relationship with the Word of God. Verses 16-17:

> 16 Let <u>the word of Christ</u> dwell in you richly <u>in all wisdom;</u> teaching and admonishing one another in psalms and hymns and spiritual songs, singing with grace in your hearts to the Lord.

17 And whatsoever ye do in word or deed, do all in the name of the Lord Jesus, giving thanks to God and the Father by him.

How blessed are we when we find other believers with whom we can fellowship; sharing our challenges and blessings. In whatever we say or do, it should be done whole-heartedly in Jesus' name with thanksgiving.

He moves on to give instructions regarding specific relationships. He begins with the family which is the very core of God's Creation. The following verses are presented as a check list. Verses 18-22:

18 Wives, submit yourselves unto your own husbands, as it is fit in the Lord.

19 Husbands, love your wives, and be not bitter against them.

20 Children, obey your parents in all things: for this is well pleasing unto the Lord.

21 Fathers, provoke not your children to anger, lest [for fear that] they be discouraged.

22 Servants, obey in all things your masters according to the flesh; not with eye-service, as men-pleasers; but in single-ness of heart, fearing God:

These above relationships are included with his admonishing that grace believers to do every-thing wholeheartedly to the Lord. Our salvation is secure; our rewards will be according to our doing. Verses 23-25:

23 And <u>whatsoever ye do</u>, do it heartily, as to the Lord, and not unto men; **24** Knowing that of the Lord ye shall re-ceive the reward of the inheritance: for ye serve the Lord Christ.

25 <u>But he that doeth</u> wrong shall receive for the wrong which he hath done: and there is no respect [partiality] of per-sons.

Since our salvation is eternally secure, he is speak-ing about consequences of our sinful actions while we remain on earth in our fleshly bodies.

5

Colossians 4

Paul seems to add a collection of thoughts as finishing this letter. He continues with his instructions concerning relationships. In the last chapter, he finished with employees. Now, he adds his instruction for employers. Colossians 4:1:

> 1 **Masters, give unto your servants that which is just and equal; knowing that ye also have a Master in heaven.**

Employers are to treat their subordinates fairly and justly as Christ, Who is their Master, treats them.

Paul moves to the need for grace believers to pray, be watchful, and give thanks to God. There should be an open communication between the believer and God. He requests that, in their prayers, they remember his ministry which is constantly under attack by the enemy. Verses 2-4:

> 2 **Continue in prayer, and watch in the same with thanksgiving;**
>
> 3 **Withal [Along with this] praying also for us, that God would open unto us a door of utterance, to speak the mystery of Christ, for which I am also in bonds: 4 That I may make it manifest, as I ought to speak.**

Paul is always looking for an opportunity to present itself to share the good news of salvation.

Next, Paul begins to address the *walk* or the *manner of living* for grace believers in a world filled with the unsaved. The word *redeemed* means *buying back*. He is saying what time we have should not be wasted but put to good use. Verse 5:

> 5 **Walk in wisdom toward them that are without [outside the faith], redeeming the time.**

Knowing that *wisdom* is from God, Paul is referring to Scripture. Grace believers should apply the Word of God in their daily lives. Salt is a seasoning that makes things more palatable or more acceptable. Our manner of speech should be gracious and well received regardless to whom we speak. Verse 6:

> 6 Let your speech be alway with grace, seasoned with salt, that ye may know how ye ought to answer every man.

His letters usually included personal greetings, well wishes, or comments to individuals. He informed them of his own affairs and inquired about theirs. His familiarity with the Colossians and the problems with heretics troubling them was the reason for this letter. With a fatherly tone, he now addresses specific individuals. Verses 7-9:

> 7 All my state [circumstances] shall Tychicus declare unto you, who is a beloved brother, and a faithful minister and fellowservant in the Lord:

> 8 Whom I have sent unto you for the same purpose, that he might know your estate [circumstances], and comfort your hearts;

> 9 [Along] With Onesimus, a faithful and beloved brother, who is one of you. They shall make known unto you all

things which are done here.

News of their circumstances or state of affairs would be exchanged between the two parties bringing both of them up to date.

Paul names individuals who share in his ministry and exchanges greetings. Verses 10-15:

> 10 **Aristarchus my fellow-prisoner saluteth [greets] you, and Marcus, sister's son to Barnabas, (touching [concerning] whom ye received commandments [instruction]: if he come unto you, receive him;) 11 And Jesus, which is called Justus, who are of the circumcision [Jews]. These only are my fellow-workers unto the kingdom of God, which have been a comfort unto me.**

> 12 **Epaphras, who is one of you, a servant of Christ, saluteth you, always labouring fervently for you in prayers, that ye may stand perfect and complete in all the will of God. 13 For I bear him record, that he hath a great zeal for you, and them that are in Laodicea, and them in Hierapolis. 14 Luke, the beloved physician, and Demas, greet you.**

15 Salute [Greet] the brethren which are in Laodicea, and Nymphas, and the church which is in his house.

Many theologians believe that it was Epaphras who established the believers in Colossae and Laodicea. Notice that Luke, the beloved physician and writer of the Gospel of Luke as well as the Acts of the Apostles, is included as being with Paul at the time of this writing.

All of Paul's letters were written with the intention they would be read aloud before the congregation. Today, they should be read from the pulpit for instruction and edification of the believers. Although they were written to the grace believers in Colossae, these letters were shared with believers in neighboring cities such as Laodicea. These epistles are now part of the canon of Scripture and shared with all. Verses 16-17:

16 And when this epistle is read among you, cause that it be read also in the church of the Laodiceans; and that ye likewise read the epistle from Laodicea.

17 And say to Archippus, Take heed to the ministry which thou hast received in the Lord, that thou fulfil it.

It is believed that Paul wrote more letters than those included in Scripture. He mentions an epistle from Laodicea above. However, it is the wisdom of the Holy Spirit Who caused them not to be included.

Before he comes to the salutation, there is something about Paul's physical state you should know. He refers to an infirmity in his letters. In a letter to the Corinthians, he calls it a *thorn in the flesh*. 2 Corinthians 12:7-9:

> 7 And lest [for fear that] I should be exalted above measure through the abundance of the revelations, there was given to me a <u>thorn in the flesh</u>, the messenger of Satan to buffet me, lest [for fear that] I should be exalted above measure.
>
> 8 For this thing I besought the Lord thrice [three times], that it might depart from me. 9 And he said unto me, My grace is sufficient for thee: for my strength is made perfect in weakness.

The Lord decided that Paul should suffer from an infirmity or physical condition which many believe was related to his eyes. Therefore, it became necessary for him to dictate his letters to a scribe, also called an *amanuensis* who would write the manuscript on Paul's behalf.

There was concern about false letters being produced and sent to the churches as being from Paul. Therefore, he would write in his own hand at the end of his letters. Here are three verses which support this fact. 1 Corinthians 16:21:

> **21 The salutation of me Paul with mine own hand.**

We see it in Galatians 6:11:

> **11 Ye see how large a letter I have written unto you with mine own hand.**

2 Thessalonians 3:17:

> **17 The salutation of Paul with mine own hand, <u>which is the token in every epistle: so [therefore] I write</u>.**

This may appear to be much ado about nothing, but I have a supposition or hypothesis. Paul wrote to the grace believers for whom he was the Apostle to the Gentiles. His letters to them were authenticated by his own handwriting. However, the letter to the Hebrews has no known author. Its author demonstrates an excellent knowledge of the Hebrew religion even to the level of a Pharisee. Today, that would be the same as a Doctor of Law. Scripture is only written by someone who is ordained and inspired by God. Not just anyone can be included in the canon of Scripture. In the New Testament, it would have to be an apostle.

Paul demonstrated his burden for his own people, Israel, in Romans 9:2-5:

> **2 That I have great heaviness and continual sorrow in my heart. 3 For I could wish that myself were accursed from Christ for my brethren, my kinsmen according to the flesh:**
>
> **4 Who are Israelites; to whom pertaineth the adoption, and the glory, and the covenants, and the giving of the law, and the service of God, and the promises; 5 Whose are the fathers, and of whom as concerning the flesh Christ came, who is over all, God blessed for ever. Amen.**

It is my belief that Paul wrote the book Hebrews. He did not sign the letter because he did not want it to be viewed as intended for those saved by grace. The book of Hebrews is the first book following Paul's letters. Those that following his are considered as the Jewish epistles. Peter, the Apostle to the Circumcision (Gal. 2:7-8), wrote this to the Jews who believed the Kingdom Gospel preached by Jesus and His twelve disciples. 2 Peter 3:15-16:

> **15 And account that the longsuffering of our Lord is salvation; even as <u>our beloved brother Paul</u> also according to the wisdom given unto him <u>hath written unto you;</u>**

> **16 As also in all his epistles, speaking in them of these things; in which are some things hard to be understood, which they that are unlearned and unstable wrest [twist], <u>as they do also the other scriptures</u>, unto their own destruction.**

Did the above just confirm that Paul wrote to the Jews? It would appear so. It would make sense that Paul did not sign a letter intended for his beloved brethren creating confusion for grace believers.

In view of the above, we can understand the significance of the closing of his letter. Colossians 4:18:

18 The salutation <u>by the hand of me</u>
Paul. Remember my bonds. Grace be
with you. Amen.

6

Philemon 1

There are two good reasons commentators include Colossians and Philemon together. First, Philemon is a very short letter with only one chapter. Second, both Philemon and Onesimus were connected to the believers in Colossians. At the time of the New Testament, it is believed there were 120 million inhabitants in the Roman Empire of which 60 million were slaves. Today, the concept of slavery is an anathema. However, it was a common practice during the time of this epistle.

The letter to Philemon is about two men. Philemon lived in Colossae. He is a wealthy man who owns slaves. The other man, Onesimus, is one of his slaves and considered to be property. Onesimus escaped and fled to Rome where, by divine intervention, he later met the Apostle to the Gentiles. It is interesting that his name, *Onesimus*, means *useful* and that is exactly what he became for the purpose of the gospel. Hearing Paul preach the Gospel of Grace, Onesimus believes and is saved by grace through faith. During Paul's incarceration in Rome, Onesimus becomes *useful* to Paul and helps to meet his needs. He becomes aware, probably by Onesimus' confession, that he is a runaway slave. This letter is written to Philemon who is a grace believer in the Colossian church. Not only is he a believer, but the church is also meeting in his house.

Onesimus is the scribe who writes Paul's words. To add a splash of drama, he is also the one who will deliver this letter to Philemon, his master. Philemon 1:1-3:

> 1 **Paul, a prisoner of Jesus Christ, and Timothy our brother, unto Philemon our dearly beloved, and fellowlabourer, 2 And to our beloved Apphia, and Archippus our fellowsoldier, and to the church in thy house: 3 Grace to you, and peace, from God our Father and the Lord Jesus Christ.**

Since the recipient of this letter is an individual, Paul uses the singular pronouns of *thee* and *thou*. In other words, he is not addressing a group of believers.

However, the contents of the letter were *useful* enough to include in the canon of Scripture. Verses 4-7:

> 4 I thank my God, making mention of thee always in my prayers, 5 Hearing of thy love and faith, which thou hast toward the Lord Jesus, and toward all saints;
>
> 6 That the communication of thy faith may become effectual by the acknowledging of every good thing which is in you in Christ Jesus.
>
> 7 For we have great joy and consolation in thy love, because the bowels [inner most parts] of the saints are refreshed by thee, brother.

Now, Paul gets to the heart of the letter which is to *enjoin* Philemon to do something. The word *enjoin* used below is *a request that carries with it authority.* Verses 8-9:

> 8 Wherefore, though I might be much bold in Christ to enjoin thee that which is convenient [appropriate], 9 Yet for love's sake I rather beseech thee, being

such an one as [me] Paul the aged, and now also a prisoner of Jesus Christ.

Picture this. Onesimus is standing before Philemon. Your runaway slave has not only returned, but he has with him a letter from the Apostle Paul.

Paul gets right to the point and makes his request. Verses 10-13:

> 10 **I beseech [ask with a sense of urgency] thee for my son Onesimus, whom I have begotten in my bonds: 11 Which in time past was to thee unprofitable, but now profitable to [both] thee and to me:**
>
> 12 **Whom I have sent again: thou therefore receive him, that is, mine own bowels [my inner most parts]: 13 Whom I would [rather] have retained with me, that in thy stead [place] he might have [otherwise] ministered unto me in the bonds of the gospel:**

Like Timothy, Paul considers Onesimus as his son in the faith helping him in his imprisonment while Paul taught him. Onesimus would bear the fruit of Paul's labors in him. According to Greek Orthodox tradition, Onesimus became the Bishop of Byzantium, which later became Constantinople. It is now Istanbul, Turkey.

In the above verses, Paul refers to Philemon's financial cost of losing a slave–a valuable possession. But, he declares it to be gain for both of them for the ministry of the Gospel of Grace. In spite of his personal need for Onesimus' assistance, Paul makes it clear he will only accept Onesimus' service if Philemon returns him willingly. Verse 14:

> **14 But without thy mind [approval] would I do nothing; that thy benefit should not be as it were of necessity, but willingly.**

However, should Philemon decide to keep him, he should do so not as a slave or servant, but as a fellow grace believer in Christ. Verse 15:

> **15 For perhaps he therefore departed for a season [a while], that thou shouldest receive him for ever; 16 Not now as a servant, but above a servant, a brother beloved, specially to me, but how much more unto thee [to receive him back], both in the flesh, and in the Lord?**

As mentioned previously, Philemon was a leader among the believers in Colossae. Paul, our pattern or example, follows Christ. He asks that Philemon receive Onesimus back as he would receive Paul himself. If there is any debt owed, he asks Philemon to put it on his account and he will repay him. Verses 17-19:

> 17 **If thou count me therefore a partner, receive him [Onesimus] as myself. 18 If he hath wronged thee, or oweth thee ought [anything], put that on mine account;**

> 19 **I Paul have written it with mine own hand, I will repay it: albeit [in view of all] I do not say to thee how thou owest unto me even thine own self besides.**

He concludes by saying that he will repay Philemon for any loss he incurred from Onesimus. Then, he continues by making the point that Philemon's own salvation was due to Paul. I think he wanted Philemon to think on that.

The word *bowels* means *the innermost part* of someone's being. He deeply hopes that Philemon will receive Onesimus with grace, forgiving him as he himself was forgiven, and return him to Paul to continue in service to the Lord. Verses 20:

> 20 **Yea, brother, let me have joy of [from] thee in the Lord: refresh my bowels [inner most parts] in the Lord.**

In the following verse, Paul speaks of *obedience* but it implies his *obedience to the faith.* This is done by remembering the faith and by its genuine application. Verse 21:

> 21 **Having confidence in thy obedience I wrote unto thee, knowing that thou wilt also do more than I say [ask].**

It is Paul's desire to see the grace believers in Colossae face to face. I am sure he writes this to let Philemon know that, at some point, he may see Paul in person again. Verse 22:

> 22 **But withal prepare me also a lodging: for I trust that through your prayers I shall be given [brought] unto you.**

As with the closing of his other letters, he mentions individuals. There are people within the group of grace believers in which he exchanges greetings. Verses 23-24:

23 There salute thee Epaphras, my fellowprisoner in Christ Jesus; 24 Marcus, Aristarchus, Demas, Lucas, my fellowlabourers.

He closes the letter with the following blessing in verse 25:

25 The grace of our Lord Jesus Christ be with your spirit. Amen.

Epilogue

These two letters reveal the interpersonal dynamics that the Apostle Paul has with his *children of faith.* Like a caring parent, he continually prays for and anguishes over them as offspring left in the wilds of this present world. He continues his relationship with them up until his death in circa 64 AD.

He writes to encourage them, to confirm doctrine, or refute false doctrine. In Galatia, it was the Judaizers who wanted to add the keeping of the Mosaic Law as part of the requirements for salvation by grace through faith. In Colossae, it was the influence of pagan religions and the vain philosophies of man. There was a significant challenge made to the full deity and full humanity of Christ. These two threats continue today in Christian churches. Nothing has changed. Therefore, Paul's response still applies.

Philemon is an excellent book to end the collection of Pauline epistles. It is perfect because it is a simple example of grace applied! Think about the situation of Onesimus. Can each of us identify with his circumstances? All of us were slaves to sin before our salvation–before we were saved by grace through faith. We heard the gospel and believed God's gracious offer. We were redeemed by the blood–bought back as a captive to sin and freed. In view of Onesimus' continued involvement, it appears that Philemon exercised grace and released his former slave who, now, is his brother.

The Gospel of Grace is offered to all people without distinction. However, only those who believe the effectiveness of Christ's death, burial, and resurrection applies to them, will be saved. Christ's atonement is sufficient for all, but only efficient or effective for those who choose to believe.

—Dr. David Alan Greene

Other GraceWord Publications

Cartas A Teófilo
Efesios: Dispensacionalmente considerado
El evangelio Oculto: Una vez fue un misterio . . .

About The Author

Dr. David Alan Greene has over thirty-five years of experience as an insurance agent selling both property and casualty as well as life insurance. During his career, he taught and explained the content and meaning of policies to his clients. Now retired, he devotes much of his time to teaching the Bible.

He obtained his Bachelor of Theology, Master of Biblical Studies, and Ph.D. in Biblical Studies from Evangelical Theological Seminary where he holds the position of Dean of Graduate Studies. He also holds a Ph.D. in Christian Counseling. He has written numerous biblical commentaries and books on rightly dividing the Word of Truth.

www.ingramcontent.com/pod-product-compliance
Lightning Source LLC
Chambersburg PA
CBHW070803120626
46557CB00002B/694